MW00936351

Journaling Basics –

Journal Writing for Beginners

Lisa Shea

Cover design by Lisa Shea
Book design by Lisa Shea
Visit my website at <u>LisaShea.com</u>

Amazon: B00MHXC3FI
Lulu: 978-1-312-41679-6
SmashWords 9781311916303

~ 4 ~

First Printing: August 2014

All author's proceeds of the Journaling series benefit
battered women's shelters.

I am not a medical doctor. Please consult a trained
professional before you attempt any life changes or if you
have discomfort.

Every day is a new adventure.

Reach for your dreams!

Journaling Basics

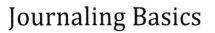

Table of Contents

Introduction

The first sentence can't be written
Until the first sentence is written.
-- Joyce Carol Oates, WD

Journals. The word brings to mind something mystical and magical, something which unlocks the hidden secrets within us and releases a new blossoming of power and strength. Perhaps we imagine curling up on a velvet cushion against a sun-streaked window, pouring our thoughts out into a leather-bound diary. Maybe we dream of sprawling beneath a large oak tree, unfolding our glorious future. Maybe what we need right now is simply a laptop, a few moments of quiet, and the ability to release the pain and hurt which has for so long been trapped within us.

It is all journaling.

There are countless books out there that will insist journaling is only right if it's done the author's way. A journal must follow, exactly, a specific method. A journal must be done in a certain kind of book or binder. Each page must be laid out a precise manner. Authors will tell you that journals aren't diaries. Journals aren't letters to yourself. Journal's aren't – aren't – aren't.

I've been journaling for nearly forty years – from when I was quite a tiny girl. It seemed natural to me to write down my thoughts, hopes, and dreams in order to process and organize them. What I've found in all these years of experiments, explorations, and extravaganzas is that only *you* can say what journaling means to you.

We are all different people. We all have different needs. We come from different backgrounds and we relate to different techniques.

Some people thrive with three-ring binders. That's great! Others adore the feel of laptop keys beneath their fingers. Some like a strict schedule of writing for thirty minutes each evening about what the day held and their thoughts on that day. Others favor a free approach of writing whatever, whenever, however.

That's OK.

This journal is for *you*. Not for some distant author; not for the family member who may never truly understand you. It's for you and you alone. Therefore the only important thing to figure out is which style works best for you. There are no rules to break. There are no mandates to chafe against. This is all about you. It's about releasing your fears, easing stress points, and creating a smooth flow in your life so that you can achieve your dreams and find the serenity that you deserve.

It all begins with this one step.

Let's get started on the delightful, warm, soul-enriching world of journals!

Lisa's Note:

You'll hear the following message throughout this book: I feel strongly that only *you* can decide what is best for you. This is true in so many ways. That being said, I imagine part of why you picked up this book is you're curious about my point of view on things. I've been journaling for decades and you'd like to know what I've found works for me.

Therefore, I'll include my own preferences at the end of many chapters here. Please keep in mind that just because they work for me doesn't mean they're right for you! Sure, give them a try if you wish, but also be open to the alternatives. It's only through trial runs that we determine what works best for us.

I am extremely open to all feedback and ideas on improving this information. I post regularly about writing and self-expression on my various social networking sites, so the process of learning is ongoing. Together we help each other thrive.

I feel strongly about helping battered women's shelters (the cause this project supports). The more we improve the book's message of self-exploration, the more we help ourselves and others!

What Is Journaling?

Put simply, journaling is the act of you recording your thoughts on something. It could be the day's events, like a diary. It could be thoughts on a book you've read. It might be memories of a dream. Perhaps it's your hopes for your future. All of that and more is journaling.

The word "journal" comes from the Latin word *diurnalis*. The root of this word means "daily." The diurnalis was the book that tracked the times people said their prayers each day. So in a way it was a diary. Soon this document took on more life, recording things other than those prayers.

Journaling has been done since humans learned to write, and many famous people have enjoyed journaling. Leonardo da Vinci kept a notebook. Anne Frank's thoughts provide a poignant view into her too-short life. Bob Dylan liked to jot down ideas. Matsuo Basho, famous for his haiku, kept journals of his travels.

Your journaling can open up a wonderful new world to you!

Journaler vs Journalist

While it might seem that a "journalist" is someone who journals, the word journalist is already strongly associated with a professional who writes for a newspaper. This is generally a different type of writing from someone who is keeping a private journal.

For that reason, many journalers prefer the title "journaler" or simply "writer." It helps keep that distinction clear.

You can call yourself whatever you wish! Labels in life can be so challenging. Go with what makes you happy.

Non-Electronic Journaling

A book is simply the container of an idea –
Like a bottle, what is inside the book is what matters.
-- Angela Carter

A journal is, at its core, a collection of your thoughts, ideas, ruminations, ponderings, tantrums, aspirations, and more. It is the innermost part of you pouring out so you can poke at it, ponder it, and make some sense out of the jigsaw puzzle pieces.

We all have our styles we enjoy. Sometimes we've been trained one way by our parents or teachers and don't even realize that we would vastly prefer something else until we try it. So I suggest testing out each of these methods for a week or more.

Give it a chance. Let yourself get through the initial settling process. There's no rush here.

Journaling is something that stays with you for your entire life.

Even if you're an experienced writer, it might be a great time to start a fresh set of experiments. Sometimes we can get stuck in a rut or too used to the way things have always been. Experimenting at different stages of our life can reap great rewards.

Always be open to change!

Finding the ideal – for you – journaling setup can mean the difference between falling in love with journaling and abandoning it out of frustration. For those who have journaled in the past, it can revitalize your passion.

Let's start with a variety of non-electronic options for journaling. It's a good idea to experiment with and come to be familiar with these styles. They will serve you well even when batteries run dead, when a snowstorm takes out your power, and when you simply wish to unplug.

Small Notepad

Small notepads are the simplest of all writing systems. Even the Greeks and Romans would write by hand on a small, hand-held surface. In those days they would prepare a wood backing with a layer of wax on it. They'd use a stylus to make marks in that wax. Then, when they had their thoughts set, they'd transcribe it to more permanent parchment with ink. They'd wipe clean the wax and start again!

The idea here is that you keep this notepad on you most of the time. Have a thought? You can scribble it down. Something keeping you awake at night? Grab the notepad from your headboard and release the images from your tired brain.

Many times, even if you have another primary method of journaling, having that little notepad around as a back-up measure can be incredibly valuable. There are times that something important will come up that you crave writing about and your normal journal just isn't around. The more you're able to write when you crave writing, the easier the writing process gets the rest of the time.

I keep a notebook on my headboard for those late night thoughts. I keep one in my purse for thoughts I might have while going about my daily chores. There's one in the car's glove compartment, too.

When I go out on photography trips I keep a notebook to record any particular thoughts about lighting or settings for a shot. Especially with my film cameras, this can come in quite handy later on.

One downside to the small notepad is that it's not very secure. Anybody who happens across it can page through your thoughts. For people who live alone this might not be a major concern. For those with house-mates, this could be far trickier.

Still, I highly recommend you keep a few small notebooks in your life.

Spiral Bound Notebooks

The larger sibling of a small notepad, many people consider spiral bound notebooks as a staple of their school years. The pages all stay in order. They're usually lined, although you can get them plain or with grids.

Spiral-bound notebooks keep everything organized and in one spot. If you create a page that you feel is a mistake, you can rip out that page and it's as if it never existed. There's no remnant of its presence.

Spiral-bound notebooks can be quite cheap. For those on a budget, that's a great benefit. The cover can easily be decorated with doodles, stickers, photos, and other decorations.

As you experiment with spiral-bound notebooks, you might realize that, for you, they are simply not very appealing. They may not draw you in to write. They might actually make you discouraged from writing, because all that comes to mind is unhappy times being picked on in school.

So while a spiral bound notebook might be quite functional, and quite inexpensive, it also may not be the best choice for you. For others, it could be absolutely perfect. It could remind them of discipline and order.

I use spiral-bound notebooks for art journals.

Give it a try and see if spiral notebooks are good for the stage you're in!

3-Ring Binders

Some people swear by 3-Ring Binders for storing all sorts of things – car maintenance records, house maintenance records, and journals. They can divide their journal pages up by sections. They can keep multiple binders for multiple journaling projects. They can rearrange pages to make more sense. They can add in sleeves with additional photos and material to supplement the written record.

I have an entire shelf of my office taken up by 3-ring binders. My car maintenance book tracks all work done on my car. I've made a 3-ring binder for the art group I belong to, so each member has a page promoting them and their artwork. A visitor to one of our events can page through and learn more about all of us.

3-Ring binders are, indeed, incredibly versatile.

Some would argue that this means the organic flow of the conversation is lost. Switching things around might lose the original track of the thoughts. Of course, then you could number the pages, but now you're introducing something that might get lost or confused.

If the pages are simply bound and stuck in an order there's no question of how the progression goes. The order goes 1-2-3. But for some people, that stuck-with-life issue is one they're trying to overcome. To them, the cast-in-stone nature of a spiral binder would discourage them from journaling at all. The freedom of a three-ring, where thoughts can easily be rearranged and worked with, might be just what they crave.

Bound Journals

Here we go. The classic. Bound journals come in a wide array of shapes, sizes, and colors, Many people lust after and collect journals as others might collect shoes or shot glasses. There are just so many to choose from! Leather tooled. Fabric covered. Journals made from recycled paper. Journals featuring your favorite book character.

I've tried all of these journal types over the years, and I find for my most personal thoughts that I always come back to a pretty, bound journal. I have quite a number of them. I can look through my old journals and remember where I was in life based on its color and texture. It brings me joy to pick up my journal and work on it.

Then again, the years I was on a tight budget, I was thrilled to have *any* way to journal my thoughts and keep myself on an even keel. I was quite content to do it on my laptop where it was free. I could write pages after pages and never run out.

A bound journal can come with a lock, but most are open to whoever picks them up. With its attractive shape, it might lure more people than usual to come see what's within it.

Typewriters

I thought I'd include this category for fun, because I do know several writers who adore typewriters and feel they do their best work with them. There's something about the feel of the keys beneath the finger and the soothing, rhythmic sound. I suppose it's like the difference of playing a grand piano vs a modern keyboard.

Some writers even put a long, continual-sheet roll of paper into a typewriter and just typed and typed. It never stopped. There was never an "end of a page." The writer could keep going on until they reached the end of their roll!

If are a typewriter fanatic, embrace it! If you haven't touched a typewriter in years (or ever) see if you have any friends who have one. Give it a try and see what you think.

Lisa's Thoughts

I wholeheartedly recommend embracing all of the options shown here – except, perhaps, the typewriter.

Keep small notebooks on you. Use 3-ring binders to organize information they're best suited for. Have a few bound journals in your bedroom. Each of these systems becomes ideal for a certain type of recording.

As I mentioned, my most personal connection is with bound journals. I have them on shelves beside my bed and it's soothing to look over at them and know all my hopes, fears, and dreams are there within easy reach.

They're primarily leather and cloth bound. I seem to be drawn to those. I love the texture of them in my hands. I like the weight of them. I love the feel of the gel pen against the paper.

That being said, I wouldn't want to carry one around with me all day in my purse. By having a mix of options, you're best able to face whatever the day throws at you.

So, for me, that diversity of choices is what works best.

Lined / Unlined / Grid

It might seem like such a simple question. What type of markings – if any – should your journal have in it to begin with?

The book you write in can have guidelines to keep you organized. It could have grid lines to be even more formal and logical. It could have decorative flowers or flourishes along the edges.

Or your book could have completely blank pages. Blank, vacant, staring at you.

The possibilities are fairly endless, especially if you choose to journal on a computer system or in a 3-Ring binder. Heck, you could change your line style on a daily basis!

This is an area where you should definitely experiment. Lines might appeal to you at first – but you might find that you enjoy the freedom to sway and draw, to write large and small as the mood strikes you.

On the other hand, you might find that having a big, blank page with nothing at all on it intimidates you. You might find that the lines seem warm, welcoming, and encourage you to fill them in.

It might also be that you enjoy one style for several years and then decide you'd like to try the other for a few. We all change and grow. Just because you've done it one way in the past, don't feel you should be stuck. Be willing to experiment and try new options, just to change things up.

You could even have multiple journals at your beck and call. One lined for your more formal thoughts. One unlined for when you're feeling creative. Try laying both out before you as you embark on a journaling session. Which do you reach for? Does the way you journal change based on that option?

Whatever you go with, it's one step along your path. You can always change in the future.

Lisa's Thoughts

I use lined journals with wide lines. That way I have space to write and it keeps my writing fairly easy to read later on.

I do have drawing pads that I use for journaling when I'm feeling more creative.

I have many pads with grid lines but I tend to feel that I need to "save" them for a special occasion. And then I never end up using them. I should just go wild and use them anyway.

I should call each day special.

The Writing Implement

Just as important as choosing what you want to write *in* is what implement you'll best be suited to write *with*.

This question isn't as obvious as it might sound! There are a variety of choices out there. Each one has its pros and cons. Each one creates a different emotional feel in your mind which could change the way your thoughts flow.

An implement isn't extraneous to the process of journaling. It's an important component of the activity. Just like writing in a noisy coffeehouse might result in different thoughts being written down compared with writing at a mountain-top Zen retreat in the middle of a beautiful autumn weekend.

So be mindful of what you choose to write with. Let's go through just a few of the options available.

Pencil

Many people adore the feel of a soft, graphite pencil sliding smoothly across the surface of paper. It's soothing, welcoming, reminding them of childhood or better times.

Did you know that pencils were *never* made from lead? In the 1500s, when graphite was discovered, people thought it was a type of lead. So pencil-makers then called the pencils they made "lead pencils" even though they were always technically graphite pencils.

One of a pencil's great traits is that the marks it makes can be erased. Whatever you write, if you wish to, you can cause them to vanish away again. Nothing is carved in stone. Everything can be changed. This can be quite freeing for those who worry about "getting it right."

On the down side, some people find writing with pencil to be more physically challenging than writing with a smooth gel pen.

Also, pencils need sharpening occasionally, unless you get a mechanical pencil which will always stay sharp for you.

I'm one of those people who finds the "drag" of the pencil on the paper to be slowing. That being said, I love drawing with pencil. So if I'm doing an art journal entry, often I prefer pencil.

Colored Pencil

Ah, one of my favorites. I adore colored pencils. They create amazing shades. You can switch between them as you write, illustrating clearly your thoughts. If you're doing out a to-do list, you can make each type of task a different color. There are a wealth of ways in which you can use colored pencils.

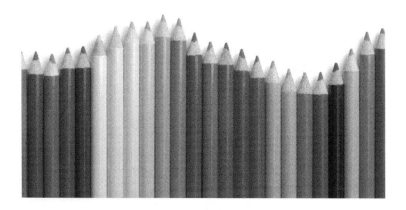

The downsides here are much the same as with regular pencils. You have to sharpen them. They might not be as free-flowing as a gel pen would be. And with the colored versions, they tend to be harder to erase. So you lose some of the flexibility that you have with a simple graphite pencil.

Pen

A pen comes with a permanent feel. It's like doing a crossword puzzle in pen. It commits you to something. It gives you the sense that your words won't be lost or erased. They won't fade as much over time. You can come back in ten or twenty years and ponder how you felt.

If you write in pen, be sure to test out different types of pens. Gel pens can flow much more smoothly than ballpoints. I adore gel pens with "squishy" barrels. Often when I lend those to a friend they never return to me. That's all right! I love to share the joy.

Pens come in different colors! Try having a selection available and see if sometimes you decide you want to write in something unusual.

For my evening bound journals, I have a collection of colored gel pens by my bed. That way I can write in whatever color calls to me.

Calligraphy Pen

I'll put calligraphy pens into their own category because they are just so cool. I love doing calligraphy on cards each Christmas. It's one of those skills that comes in handy in so many different ways.

Calligraphy ties you into an ancient tradition. It gives you that sense of history. You can imagine famous figures from hundreds of years ago sitting down with pen and ink to record their thoughts. It might not be the carving of a quill feather to dip into ink, but it's fairly close.

Consider experimenting with calligraphy. It's a powerful connection with our past. It's also a talent that becomes useful in a wide variety of situations.

Crayon

A kid's toy? Ah, but maybe that's just what you need to release your inner emotions. Give it a try. Get yourself a big box that has all the odd colors in it – hot magenta, magic mint, dandelion, and teal blue. Sometimes just the color names can be inspirational.

Allow yourself the freedom to explore and have fun.

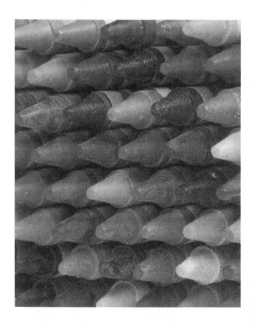

Once you release those long-held restrictions, you might find you write things you never would have thought of otherwise.

This is definitely an area where even experienced journalers might stop, shake off their old routine, and discover something fun and new.

Lisa's Thoughts

I adore my squishy UniBall 207 pens. They have a soft grip which is wonderful for my fingers. The ink flows *so* smoothly.

My boyfriend buys these for me regularly because when my friends try them out they adore them – so I give them away. I want to spread the love.

I do love all the other options, though. I use colored pens for my nighttime journals. I use colored pencils for artwork. Crayons are playful!

Be sure to explore all the options. Even if you settled on mechanical pencils years ago, do a fresh sweep and test out each style. You might find that your creativity is inspired when you do.

Electronic Journaling

We live in an amazing modern age where new devices and options are released every year. Where our grandparents might have been stuck with only physical or mechanical options, our modern-day world provides a dizzying array of fun ways to keep track of our thoughts.

We can easily combine typewritten words, audio files, photos, and video files together to create a multi-sensory journal.

Here are just a few of the options available.

Smartphone / Small Tablet

What an amazing little device! A smartphone or tablet can usually be security locked against unwanted readers. You can download all sorts of useful software to help you organize your writing. You can write anywhere, any time. You can write while you wait for the bus or as you take the train to work.

These devices can hold immense amounts of data. You could easily store years of journal entries on one small device. That could easily equate to shelves and shelves of books. If you want to refer back to what you were thinking about ten years ago, a few flicks of the finger can bring that information up – even if you're sitting on a bus to school.

On the down side, your electronic device might tempt thieves far more than a little notebook would. So there's often more stress involved in carrying a device around with you. Where you might be fine leaving a notebook on the beach towel when you jumped in the water for a while, you could be more hesitant to leave your new Apple iPad there.

There's also the system-failure data-loss issue. If you don't back up your data somewhere safe, and your device has a hiccup, you could lose that information forever. Systems do crash and die.

Also, for many people there is something powerful about moving the hand to write things down. Typing just doesn't create the same emotional connection.

Of course, for others they would far rather type than write. So this is an area where experimenting with your devices will help you see which you prefer.

There are many times that I send myself notes with my smartphone so I don't lose track of an important piece of information. If I am writing about an event or situation I'm present at, I can easily take photos to illustrate my notes.

For example, here I am in Rome, Italy with my sister. I wanted to travel as light as possible, so I had no notebook with me, but my handy smartphone was always at my side.

Large Tablet / Laptop

Keyboard-based tablets and laptops have the convenience of being what many of us are used to typing on for long hours at a stretch. Often the words flow from our fingertips far faster than we could hand write them out. Auto-correct can be a blessing or a curse, depending on what it tries to "fix" for you.

If you're traveling, a laptop can allow you to maintain your normal routine without having your main PC with you. This laptop let me write extensively during a cruise around the Hawaiian islands.

Laptops are great for security – you can set multiple levels of protection on your secrets. They also are wonderful for organizing and finding things. If you want to track down that orange-stand dream you had a few years ago, a few quick searches will find it easily. It's not quite that simple with leather-bound journals.

Still, there's of course a downside. They're usually less portable than a notebook version. They're also more attractive to thieves. You have to worry about them getting wet or dropped.

Personal Computer

For many of us, we spend all day staring into the monitor of a personal computer. It has a nice, large screen to look at. It provides a keyboard with well laid out keys. The desk holds reference material easily at hand.

I work from home and I do 90% of my writing here at my desk.

The up-side is that you're probably there already. If something comes to mind, you can easily write it down. If you need something, you can easily look it up.

The down side is that it's not portable. It's stuck in that one room. If you need to travel, or if you have thoughts or ideas outside of that room, you need another option.

I absolutely use my personal computer for most of my writing all day long. It's an important part of my overall writing effort.

It's not the only one, though!

Summary

Your younger sister might treasure her nifty iPhone. Your techno-nephew might adore his super-charged laptop. Sure, listen to what they have to say. Then experiment for yourself – and choose for yourself.

What works for one person might be a disaster for another person. That's OK. There's a reason they have lots of options out there.

Do your due diligence. Practice and explore. Figure out which system works best for you.

Don't necessarily dismiss something out of hand because it's new. Allow yourself time to get over the learning curve. Everything takes time at first to master. You might realize that the new device is absolutely perfect for you once you get the hang of it.

Once you've made a decision, don't be afraid to change. Keep experimenting every once in a while to see what new options are out there.

Sure, you'll have some information in one place and some in another. That's OK. If the new format encourages you to write more often, that's all that matters. Consider the past part of your learning experiment. It's the future you're keeping an eye on.

Lisa's Thoughts

Just as with the non-electronic journal options, I use all of the various electronic devices as part of my overall writing strategy.

I write long works on my home computer all day long. That by far is the best way for me to work on those pieces. I'm writing this book on that PC, at that desk, right now.

I use my laptop in bed for writing fiction stories. It allows me to nestle into a space and lose myself.

The smartphone goes with me wherever I travel. It's been a companion on a number of trips and recorded notes that otherwise would have been lost.

Styles of Journal Writing

There are all sorts of styles you can use when writing in your journal. You can mix and match to your heart's delight!

This is *your* book.

Again, some websites and books can be quite dictatorial about "you must write *this* way on *this* topic. A travel journal can only be called a travel journal if you follow these exact ten steps."

I wholeheartedly disagree. This is your project. You can do it any way you wish.

Even if you've been journaling for years, think about each of these journaling types and how it might help you in your life. Give each one a try. It might be some don't fit well with your lifestyle, and that's ok. It could just as easily be that you suddenly realize that one is just right for you.

Here are just a few ideas for the type of writing you can do in your journal. Be sure to let me know what other styles you find to be useful!

Diary

This is the classic type of journal that we read about in books and see in movies. After she's tucked in for the night, the little girl curls up under the covers with a flashlight. Her secret diary even has a little metal key that can lock it.

My great-grandmother kept a diary during World War II. I'm fascinated each time I read it. It talks about how people thought and viewed life during this tumultuous time period.

Diaries can be wonderfully important for us when we write them, allowing us to sort through and process our emotions. The diaries can be even more insightful when we look at them years later. If you are comfortable with sharing them, they can even be interesting to later generations.

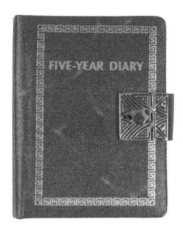

I know some diarists who burned their diaries when they got older, to ensure their emotion-laden thoughts remained private. I know others who handed their diaries down to their children as treasured insight into the lives of the older generation. It is wholly up to you, which you choose to do.

One of the most famous diaries in the world is the Diary of Anne Frank. Like many young girls, Anne was given a diary by her parents on her thirteenth birthday. Unlike most girls, though, Anne was a Jewish girl who soon was hiding with her family during World War II. She tragically ended up being killed. This diary traces her fears and hopes during that time period.

Your diary hopefully won't chronicle that same level of danger, but whatever it is you write about, it will help both you and the precious, trusted people you allow to see it.

Dream Journal

I love dream journals. Our dreams are just so full of important information for us to learn from. Our dreams are the result of our brains trying to get messages to us. If we write those messages down, we can then strive to interpret them.

A key for a dream journal is to keep it right by the bed with a pen. That way you don't have to go anywhere to get to it. You wake up, you reach for that journal, and you write. If your pen has a built in light to it, then you don't even have to turn on the light to make your notes.

The less movement you do, the more likely you are to remember most of the dream.

Also, the more that you record your dreams, the easier it becomes. You train your brain to remember them.

I adore dream journaling. Dreams have helped me learn and grow many times in my life. They have provided me with valuable lessons that I was able to examine and interpret.

If you're interested in this topic I have several books out on dreams and dream meanings. I'm also happy to chat about dreams on my various social networking feeds!

Reading Journal

Many people love to read. Often those readers draw great inspiration from what they have read. There are words and phrases which just sing to them.

Once time passes, though, it can be hard to remember the details that were amazing. This is where a reading journal comes in.

Write down those great quotes, those ideas, and other concepts that stay with you from a book. That way you can read through your notes later on and be re-inspired by what the book meant to you.

My office is filled with books, but I'd be hard pressed to remember exactly which pages my favorite parts are on in each book. A reading journal helps me find and appreciate them easily.

Hopes and Dreams Journal

Study after study shows that helps immensely to write something down. It helps firm the intention in your mind. It makes it more "real" to you so you're more likely to do the work necessary to make it happen.

I strongly advise you keep a journal about your hopes and dreams. Start by mapping out your life-long priorities, like good health or spirituality. Then decide on long-term goals that are in line with those priorities. Maybe you'd like to write a novel or earn a degree. That can then help you sort out short-term steps to help you move toward those goals.

Document what you're aiming for and the steps you'll take to get there.

One day at a time, one step at a time, and you'll make it!

I know this from personal experience. Five years ago, I didn't have my degree and I hadn't published any of my fiction novels. I was turning forty and it bothered me that these life-long dreams of mine hadn't seen progress. I'd just been too busy with "other things."

So I began journaling and laying out a plan. Just little things to get started. I researched degree options to see what was out there. I sent my novel out to friends and family to find out what they thought of it.

Step by step, piece by piece, and it all got done! I earned my Leadership degree and I've earned three awards for my novels.

You can reach your goals! Map them out and take that first step.

Travel Journal

A travel journal records all those special sights, sounds, and emotions from your trip. Sure, you can take billions of photos with your smartphone. It's still not the same as recording how you felt when you first saw that waterfall.

Travel writing has become a huge industry, as people want to take virtual vacations and explore locations from the safety of their home. Your travel journal could become the next best seller!

I absolutely adore keeping travel journals. Every time I travel I take photos, videos, and ample notes. I write everything up and post them online. That way someone else who is thinking of making that same trip can see what my experiences were, good and bad. It might help them to better prepare.

Those who are unable to travel can live vicariously through my notes, imagining that they, too, were able to visit the location.

Here's one of my photos from my trip to the Quebec ice hotel a few years ago. It was a fantastic experience, staying there overnight.

Hopefully my travel journal will encourage others to give it a try!

This is their ice chapel. There are furs laid out on the ice "pews."

Weight Loss Journal

Our modern world has created a wealth of problems for people who want to maintain a healthy weight. Foods are injected with sugars, starches, and chemicals. Our sedentary, overstressed lifestyle means we often get little exercise and eat poorly.

Maintaining a weight loss journal can help you make better choices, see patterns that you need to break, and take that first step toward a healthier you. Study after study finds that people who maintain a weight loss journal have more success in dieting in comparison with people who do not.

I run a low carb website at LowCarb.BellaOnline.com so this topic has special meaning to me. My boyfriend went from a high of 300 pounds to a low of 180 pounds through diligent effort. It happens one step at a time. One day at a time.

If you have weight loss goals, start a journal about them. You might find that it makes a noticeable difference in your progress.

Health Journal

We face so many issues in life. Cancer. MS. Alzheimer's. They can strike without warning and throw us for a loop. Often journaling is the thing that keeps us going forward.

If you're in one of these situations, write it out. Pour out your emotions and feelings. The act of writing can help you feel like you have some control over the process and reduce stress. That then leads to better health and hopefully either a faster recovery or a slower onset of symptoms.

If someone you care for has health issues, you are often put in the stressful position of being a care provider. This is also a good reason to maintain a journal. By caring for yourself, you'll become that much more capable of taking care of that person you love.

Memoir-focused Journal

While similar to a diary, a journal that is focused on a memoir project generally focuses on recording thoughts in a way that external readers can understand.

For example, if you keep your own private diary you often use a "shorthand" way of referring to things because you know their relevance. You are inside your own head.

But with a memoir, you want to connect all those dots. You want to explain why the drive-in was so important to you. You want to discuss the reasons you got emotional when you saw the first rose of the season. You want to give context to the scenes.

These types of journals can become treasured mementos for the generations that come after you. It's even better when you're able to share the thoughts while you are still around, so that you can discuss the situations with them and answer any questions that they might have.

Entrepreneur Journal

If you're thinking of running your own business, or are doing so already, it's really important to track your ups and downs. You might think that you'll remember it later, but life rarely works like that. You'll want to record it as it happens, so nothing is lost.

You want to be able to learn from your mistakes, so you avoid making them again. You'll also want to capitalize on your successes! The more you tweak and hone what works and doesn't work, the better success you'll find.

I keep journals on all my projects and I find the information invaluable. Often I don't realize a trend occurs until I go back and look for patterns. By keeping track of details over time, you create the raw data that you can use to thrive despite whatever life throws at you.

Life is about change. The world will always be changing around you. By mapping out your ups and downs, you find the path of success through all of that.

School Journal

Many students are assigned a project to keep a journal. It's training in how to write each day – how to build and maintain a creative flow.

Sometimes the journal assignment is open-ended and allows you to write on any topic you wish. At other times the journal is about a specific task – watching the leaves change colors or watching tadpoles grow their cute little arms and legs.

Yes, they are just that cute. Look at those little eyes :).

Part of the key here is to set aside time each day to work on it. That way you don't miss out on what the assignment requires.

Pet Journal

If you have a pet, then I highly recommend you keep a pet journal for that pet. I find it best to have a small spiral notebook right by the cage, tank, or other area associated with the pet. That way you can make notes about what they're eating, how they are doing, and anything else you wish to track.

Often pets will hide illnesses as part of their self-defense mechanism. You'll only notice subtle changes in their eating or movement patterns. The more you make daily notes, the more likely you are to spot those changes.

Also, as much as we might wish it, no pet is immortal. Your journal might become a treasured keepsake of your pet in later years.

Pregnancy / Childhood Journal

Pregnancy and childhood journals are often written by the parents. They typically have the child's future reading in mind. It allows the child to learn more about their early days – to see what influences and environment they grew up in.

These types of journals can often include fun photos and details about the growing young child.

There can also be a separate journal kept for the parents alone, where the parents chronicle their changing emotions and thoughts as their family changes. The journal can help them process and come to terms with those myriad of changes.

Freeform Journal

Sometimes it's nice to be able to just let loose. You don't have to talk about the day's events or the book you just finished. You can let your mind wander and wend. Explore the past. Ponder the future. Ruminate over that cabbage you saw in the garden.

A freeform journal can be greatly freeing and take you places you never dreamed possible.

Doodle. Scribble. Word-associate. Run wild with a prompt. Be creative.

The more that you allow your brain to shake out its creative juices and explore its horizons, the more your ability to problem solve and handle changes expands and grows.

Lisa's Thoughts

I have kept all of these types of journals over the years. My favorite is probably the dream journal, because I love exploring my dreams. Still, the others are quite helpful, each in their own way.

Even if you've been journaling for years, be open to shaking it up. If you've never kept a health journal, give it a try. If you haven't considered journaling your hopes and dreams, see what it's like.

You never know which style will connect with you now, regardless of your past experiences with it.

When to Write

Daily writing is an important aim in nearly all forms of journaling. As we've mentioned, the very word "diary" comes from the thought of daily writing.

Building the daily routine helps keep you on track. It becomes a normal, expected part of your day – one you look forward to and make time for.

With that being said, what part of the day should you reserve?

Morning Writing

Some people adore writing first thing in the morning, before the day takes over with all its worries and to-do lists. You can keep a journal by your bed and scribble away in it when your mind is fresh. You can sit down with a journal and your morning tea, watching the birds sing, releasing your thoughts of what's to come.

A benefit of morning writing is that it often helps you organize your thoughts for the day and set the tone of what you achieve. It's like making a to-do list – it gets your mind focused and attentive to what is to come. Often the rest of the day flows more smoothly from this start.

I have a routine where I strive to do yoga for an hour each morning. It helps my find focus and become quiet. That then serves me well for the rest of the day.

Once my yoga is complete, I map out my plans for the day. This tends to ensure that I hit the key tasks and move forward in my goals.

Mid-day Writing

With mid-day writing, it's a nice break from the surrounding activities and usually has the benefit of having you fully able to delve into the writing. For some people, they're not quite awake in the morning. They're exhausted by the evening time. It's those mid-day hours where they're most alert and able to delve into difficult topics.

It could easily be that, for you and your schedule, mid-day is simply what works. If you're racing around like a mad-person in the morning, and just sapped in the evening, it could be that mid-day provides the best option.

I am typically writing all day long, so one might say that mid-day writing is my normal style. It's when I have high energy and can make solid progress through a writing task.

Evening Writing

Evening is a delightful time to write, because the fading of the day brings a natural relaxation with it. Typically, various events have happened during the day. By setting aside time to think about them, process them, and write about them, you can put them all into context.

Often you can learn from the lessons and build on the things you've discovered.

I find evening is the best time to work on my fiction novels. I can settle into bed with my laptop, put aside the "work" of the day, and fade into my creative world.

Nighttime Writing

Journaling can be a great help in falling asleep. Often we toss and turn because we re-think conversations and worry about issues. By journaling the things through, we give them the attention they deserve.

We document them so we know they're not forgotten.

Then we can give ourselves permission to let them go for now, so our body gets the healthy rest it needs.

A key part of a nighttime journal is to agree to let the thoughts go until morning. You have sorted them. You have reviewed them. They're written down. Now your brain needs its time to rest and heal.

If you find the thoughts returning, make a few more brief notes in your journal. Then repeat to yourself that they will wait until morning. Trust in the journal to be there for you when you wake up.

Lisa's Thoughts

I in essence journal all day long. I find each stage of writing supports my life in its own way.

In the morning I organize my day and map out my plans.

During the day I record my health, my goals, my plans, and my progress.

In the evening I strive to be grateful for all I have achieved. I look for lessons in areas I had problems with and find peace.

Before I go to sleep, I do a final release of anything which is rolling around in my head. That allows me to sleep more peacefully.

Where to Write

There are just so many options about where to write. Some of us have more constraints than others, but we all have at least a few options.

Think outside the box. Be creative. See what a change of environment might do for your writing.

Here are just a few ideas to get you started.

A Different Room

Most of us have one location where we tend to write. Maybe it's a favorite chair in the living room. Maybe it's in bed. Maybe it's on the bus on the way to or from somewhere.

Shake yourself out of that routine. Try a different room. Try a different spot in the same room. Try a different book, a different writing implement, and different music while you write.

It might work, it might not work, and that's ok! That's all part of the process.

A Local Attraction

Many of us have interesting places around us to write in, and we might not even realize it. Would that café down the street allow you to hang out for an hour and sip coffee while you write? Does that library have a sunny nook where you could sit and daydream? Maybe the local museum would be more than happy for you to sit in front of a painting and see what inspiration it brought to you.

Be creative. Seek out intriguing places. If it's warm, go to your local park. If it's cold, go to a mall and people-watch. If you have friends in the area, ask if you can come over and write. No stress, no need for companionship. You just want to write somewhere new.

I love visiting local attractions. The DeCordova Sculpture Park always has fascinating things for me to look at. They can be quite inspiring to sit and stare at or to wander through. If I go with friends, it's even more fun, as we share ideas about what the various items might mean.

A Writing Retreat

While going to random locations can be quiet fun, there's something to be said to going to a place specifically set up to encourage writing. If there are other people there, you build off of each other's energy. You can share ideas and struggles.

I adored the writing retreat I attended in Vermont with a friend. It was quiet, relaxing, and just what we both needed to move forward on our projects.

If you can't afford an actual retreat, build one of your own. Set aside a day just for writing. Carve it out of your schedule just as if you were going on a trip.

If you have friends who enjoy writing, maybe you can do it as a group!

Generic Retreat

A retreat doesn't have to be geared toward writing to help your creative juices flow. One of my favorite retreats was with my stepmother to the Kripalu meditation center in western Massachusetts. It was absolutely serene with its labyrinth, gardens, and peaceful walks.

See if there are retreat options in your area. Often they provide ample quiet time for you to simply get in touch with yourself. It can be incredibly grounding and allow you greater focus and clarity going forward.

Inspirational Location

Some places simply call out with their beauty and inspiration. I vividly remember the time my sister and I visited Costa Rica. I was about to lose my frequent flier miles and I decided we would fly as far as we possibly could and explore that destination.

We stayed beneath the active volcano and soaked in the hot springs while lava trickled down its face toward us. It was quite surreal and inspiring. As you might imagine, this kind of a once-in-a-lifetime event left an indelible mark on both of our souls!

If you can't afford the trip you wish to take, make a virtual one. Hang posters on your walls. Make a recipe or two from that location. Listen to music from the place. Write about what it would be like to visit there.

Lisa's Thoughts

Anything you can do to shake up your routine is helpful for those little grey cells in your brain. We all have different challenges. Some of us are ill and are bed-ridden. We simply can't leave the bed. Some of us are stay-at-home moms with young infants who can't be left alone.

Whatever your challenge is, find a way to expand your horizons. Put new photos on the walls. Play a different kind of music. Get new candles with different aromas. Give your brain something new to process.

Writing with Prompts

A prompt is a word or phrase that gives you a starting point for your writing. It might be something as simple as "sunrise." It might be a specific situation like "first day of school." It could be an emotion – "jealousy." The idea is to give your mind a gentle jump-start and see where it goes.

There will be times that you don't want to use prompts. Maybe you had an awful day at work and you want to journal that out of your system. But on other days, your mind might feel quiet and empty. An intriguing prompt can be just what you need to spur those creative juices and see what comes out.

I definitely recommend having access to a variety of prompts on a number of topics. I have found out all sorts of fascinating things about myself by delving into prompt topics that might not have come up otherwise.

Here are a few sample prompts for you. There are of course entire books on these topics. If you have a particular topic area you want to explore, seek out a prompt book that will help with that process.

Ten Prompts on Emotions

Write the word at the top of the page. Then let your mind wander. What does it mean to you? Is it threatening? Silly? Appealing? Who do you know that embodies that word, either real or fictional?

~ True Love

~ Jealousy

~ Fear

~ Apathy

~ Guilt

~ Joy

~ Hatred

~ Hope

~ Contentment

~ Desire

Ten Prompts on Situations

If there's a situation here you haven't experienced, brainstorm what other event might have brought up similar fears and hopes.

~ First Day of School

~ First Date

~ Handling a Mean Person

~ Achieving a Goal

~ Going on a Trip

~ Listening to Great Music

~ Choosing a New Pet

~ Going Clothes Shopping

~ Being Late

~ Dealing with Family

Ten Prompts on Health

Health is one of those things that can be taken for granted until it causes issues. Find gratitude for the areas you are strong in and patience with the challenges you face.

~ Breathing

~ Weight

~ Skin

~ Hair

~ Teeth

~ Eyes

~ Pain

~ Feet

~ Energy Levels

~ Mental focus

Lisa's Thoughts

Prompts can be incredibly helpful at times. They can encourage you to delve deeply into a topic area that you might not normally write about.

For example, I did a forgiveness project where every day I journaled about a different prompt relating to forgiveness. I found that quite valuable. The lessons I learned then resonate with me today.

Handling Emotions

Journaling can let loose a pent-up dam of emotions. Sometimes a writer might not even realize they had all those emotions within them until they delved into a particular topic. That is part of the beauty of journaling. It helps to release and refresh you.

If you find you're dealing with strong emotions, give yourself room to process them. In general it is often better to release those emotions and be able to face them, rather than trying to keep them stuffed inside you. There are few times that stuffing emotions inside is healthy.

If you are at a stage where you never let anything out, then allowing that release is a critical first step.

Seeking Help

Whatever stage of life you're at, if your emotions seem overwhelming, definitely seek help. We all have times where we can be overwhelmed by life. That is what helpers are there for.

Just like a surgeon helps when we have issues with our body, there are others who can lend that help with emotional issues. It's just as important.

Your brain sends out damaging chemicals when it feels stressed. Treat your strong emotions as a medical issue just as you would a lump in your leg or other situation. It's always best to talk to someone and get assistance.

Journaling Challenges

There are always challenges with tackling a new project, and journaling is no different. It's normal and natural!

Here are issues that writers often have with journaling and ideas to overcome them. Even experienced journalers can face challenges, just as even experienced meditators can run into new hurdles in their practice.

Nothing to Write About

If you haven't been writing regularly for a while, your brain isn't in the habit of writing. Often it's not sure how to start. That's OK. That is what starting up is all about – learning the skills.

Write something. Anything. Write what happened today. Write about your favorite movie. Write about where you'd like to go on vacation.

Grab a list of prompts and choose a random one. Write whatever comes to mind about that topic.

Just write, write, write. You are training your brain and the more you practice, the easier it will get.

Too Much to Write About

Sometimes you have too much flooding your head and you don't know where to begin. So you just don't start.

Focus in on one topic. What is the most important thing that calls to you? Write just about that. Leave the rest for tomorrow. Take it one day at a time.

Too Many Distractions

We live in a world of Facebook chimes, noisy kids, ringing phones, and much more. It's hard to take a moment to think, never mind to write!

That's part of what journaling is all about. It's helping you learn coping skills for this busy world we are in.

Set your phone to mute. Set your computer to mute. Close the door. Put on noise-cancelling headphones. Just ten minutes. Find a way to carve out ten minutes to focus. This is important training for all of life.

Put a single image on your desktop computer. Focus on it. Let that focus draw you into writing.

If you haven't tried meditation or yoga, this is where they might come in helpful. They train your mind to build this ability to focus.

Painful Emotions

We are often trained by society to squelch down emotions. Men are taught not to cry. Women are taught to grin and bear it. All of those emotions don't go away. They fester until they are finally let out and allowed to cleanse.

Find support. Find friends and family who can help you through this. Talk to a professional. Do whatever it takes to help you heal and grow.

Privacy

Often when we journal we talk about issues that nobody else has ever heard about. We don't want those private thoughts to be seen by anybody.

If this is a concern to you, then research your security options and take steps. You can lock your diary up. Put passwords on your documents. Do whatever it takes so that you feel safe.

Not Enough Time

We all have time constraints which force us to struggle with too little sleep and not enough hours in the day.

Find a way to think creatively. Do an audio journal on your cell phone while you're driving. Talk to your cell in the shower. Take five minutes as you're lying in bed and trying to fall asleep.

The time exists somewhere. Seek it out. Carve out a spot. Treat that time as precious and worth protecting.

It is your own life you are working to improve. You're worth it.

Physical Challenges

Life is rarely perfect. Some of us can't see well. Some of us can't hold pens or pencils to write with them. Some of us can't sit up in a chair.

That's fine!

However it is you are dealing with the world, find a way to record your thoughts. Use an audio system rather than a written one. Use thicker crayons. Enlist a trusted friend to help out.

There's always a way. You just have to figure it out.

Self-Consciousness

Sometimes, even though we're writing private thoughts for ourselves, we're shy. We have never done this before. Committing our private thoughts to paper or computer feels unnatural and scary.

Take it slow. Start with gentle discussions. Work your way into greater revelations. You'll find it gets easier as you go – and that your stress levels reduce as you work your way through those emotions.

Summary

We have only scratched the surface of journaling here. This is a *basics* book, after all! This book is meant to give you a foundation to build on!

There are hundreds of detailed books, webpages, and other content out there which help you delve into particular areas you want to learn more about.

* Prompts for forgiveness.

* Prompts for relationships.

* Prompts for tackling projects.

* Prompts for dealing with money issues.

The key with journaling is to just do it. Find a time each day to write, and sit down.

Sometimes nothing might come to mind, so use a prompt. Other times the words will flow out of you non-stop. The more you practice, the easier it is for your mind to release those words.

It's like anything else in life. You have to get yourself into the rhythm of it.

Best of luck to you!

All author's proceeds of this journaling series benefit battered women's shelters.

If you enjoyed this book, please leave feedback on Amazon, Goodreads, and any other systems you use. Together we can help make a difference!

Be sure to sign up for my free newsletter! You'll get alerts of free books, discounts, and new releases. I run my own newsletter server – nobody else will ever see your email address. I promise!

http://www.lisashea.com/lisabase/subscribe.html

Also, be sure to check out my other related books!

Journaling Basics - Journal Writing for Beginners

Journaling Prompts - Self-Esteem

Journaling Prompts - Money and Financial Health

Journaling Prompts - Gratitude

Journaling Prompts - Forgiveness

Journaling Prompts - Love and Romance

Journaling Prompts - Getting Over a Breakup

Journaling Prompts – Weight Loss

Journaling Prompts - Procrastination

If there's another topic you'd like me to cover, please let me know. I'm happy to help!

Dedication

To the Boston Writing Group, who supports me in all my dreams.

To Ruth, who always provides awesome feedback on each of my projects!

To my boyfriend, Bob, who has brought me joy for 19 years and counting.

Most of all, to all my loyal fans on Facebook, Twitter, GoodReads, and the other systems. It is due to your support that I keep writing. I am so thrilled that this journaling series is helping so many people improve their lives.

Journals in the Movies

These are just a few of the movies that involve journals or diaries in them.

Bridget Jones' Diary

Ah, the classic. The original book was laid out as if we were sneaking peaks into this woman's actual diary. The movie carried on the idea. It made the story seem more intimate.

The Diary of Anne Frank

A movie of a very different feel. Poor tragic Anne was caught up in World War II and this real-life diary reflected the traumas she had to go through.

Dear Dumb Diary

This kid-friendly movie is about an eleven year old girl who captures all her dreams and aspirations in her diary. It reminds us how powerful a diary can be as a way of focusing in on what is important to us.

The Princess Diaries

Another teen-aimed story, this one is about a young, geeky girl who suddenly gets chosen to be a princess.

The Notebook

This romantic classic revolves around a notebook a husband has kept to help maintain a relationship with his wife, whose memory is fading.

About the Author

Lisa Shea believes strongly that each of us can overcome the obstacles in our life by diligently examining them. That is a key part of what journaling can help with.

Be patient. Take it a day at a time. Those little steps do add up!

Please visit Lisa at LisaShea.com to learn more about her background and interests. Feedback is always appreciated!

Lisa Shea has written 39 fiction books, 81 non-fiction books, and 36 short stories.

Please visit the following pages for news about free books, discounted releases, and new launches.

Feel free to post questions there – I strive to answer within a day!

Facebook:
https://www.facebook.com/LisaSheaAuthor

Twitter:
https://twitter.com/LisaSheaAuthor

Google+:
https://plus.google.com/+LisaSheaAuthor/posts

Blog:
http://www.lisashea.com/lisabase/blog/

GoodReads:
https://www.goodreads.com/author/show/6432529.Lisa_Shea

WattPad:
http://www.wattpad.com/user/lisasheaauthor

Share the news – we all want to enjoy interesting novels!

Medieval romance novels:
Seeking the Truth
Knowing Yourself
A Sense of Duty
Creating Memories
Looking Back
Badge of Honor
Lady in Red
Finding Peace
Believing your Eyes
Trusting in Faith
Sworn Loyalty
In A Glance

Each medieval novel is a stand-alone story set in medieval England. The novels can be read in any order and have entirely separate casts of characters. In comparison, the below series are each linear and connected in nature.

Cozy murder mystery series:
Aspen Allegations | Birch Blackguards | Cedar Conundrums

Sci-fi adventure romance series:
Aquarian Awakenings | Betelgeuse Beguiling | Centauri Chaos |
Draconis Discord

Dystopian journey series:
Into the Wasteland | He Who Was Living | Broken Images

Scottish regency time-travel series:
One Scottish Lass | A Time Apart | A Circle in Time

1800s Tennessee black / Native American series:
Across the River

Lisa's short stories:
Chartreuse | The Angst of Change | BAAC | Melting |
Armsby

Black Cat short stories:
Lisa's 31-book cozy mini mystery series set in Salem Massachusetts
begins with:
The Lucky Cat – Black Cat Vol. 1

Here are a few of Lisa's self-help books:

Secrets to Falling Asleep
Get Better Sleep to Improve Health and Reduce Stress

Dream Symbol Encyclopedia
Interpretation and Meaning of Dream Symbols

Lucid Dreaming Guide
Foster Creativity in a Lucid Dream State

Learning to say NO – and YES! To your Dream
Protect your goals while gently helping others succeed

Reduce Stress Instantly
Practical relaxation tips you can use right now for instant stress relief

Time Management Course
Learn to End Procrastination, Increase Productivity, and Reduce Stress

Simple Ways to Make the World Better for Everyone
Every day we wake up is a day to take a fresh path, to help a friend,
and to improve our lives.

Author's proceeds from all these books benefit battered women's
shelters.

"Be the change you wish to see in the world."

As a special treat, as a warm thank-you for buying this book and supporting the cause of battered women, here's a sneak peek at the first chapter of *Aspen Allegations*.

Aspen Allegations was awarded a 2013 Gold Medal from the Independent Publisher Book Awards.

Aspen Allegations - Chapter 1

What is life?
It is the flash of a firefly in the night.
It is the breath of a buffalo in the wintertime.
It is the little shadow which runs across the grass
and loses itself in the sunset.
~ Crowfoot, Blackfoot warrior

The woods were lovely, dark, and deep. My footfalls on the thick layer of tawny oak leaves made that distinctive crisp-crunch sound that seemed unique in all of nature. The clouds above were soft grey, cottony, a welcome relief from the torrents of Hurricane Sandy which had deluged the east coast two days earlier. Sutton had been lucky. Plum Island, Massachusetts, a mere ninety minutes northeast, had been nearly blown away by eighty-mile-an-hour winds. Here we had seen only a few downed trees, Whitins Pond once again rising over its banks, and the scattering of power outages which seemed to accompany every weather event.

I breathed in a lungful of the rich autumn air tanged with moss, turkey-tail mushroom, and the redolent muskiness of settling vegetation. Nearly all of the deciduous trees had released their weight for the year, helped along in no small part by the gale-force winds of Tuesday. That left only the pine with its greenery of five-needled bursts and the delicate golden sprawls of witch hazel blossoms scattered along the path.

It was nice to be outdoors. Two days of being cooped up in my house-slash-home-office had left me eager to stretch my legs. The Sutton Forest was far quieter than Purgatory Chasm this time of year, in no small part because hunting season had begun a few weeks earlier. The bow-and-arrow set were out stalking the white-tailed deer, and they had just been joined by those eager for coyote, weasel, and fox. I wore a bright orange sarong draped over my jacket in deference to my desire to make it through the day unperforated.

A golden shaft of sunlight streamed across the path, and I smiled at where it highlighted a scattering of what appeared to be small dusty-russet pumpkins. I stooped to pick one up, nudging its segments apart with a thumbnail. A smooth nut stood out within its center. A hickory, perhaps? I would have to look that up later when I returned home. I had finally indulged myself with a smartphone a few years ago when I turned forty, and while I liked to carry it for safety reasons, I preferred to leave it untouched when breathing in the delights of a beautiful day.

The woods were quiet, and I liked them this way. The Sutton Forest network stretched across the middle of the eight-mile-square town, but it seemed that few of the ten-thousand residents knew of this beautiful wilderness. In comparison, Purgatory Chasm, a short mile away, was usually bustling with a multi-faceted selection of humanity. Rowdy teenage boys, not yet convinced of their 'vincibility', dared each other to get closer to the edge of the eighty-foot drop into the crevasse. Cautious parents would climb along its boulder-strewn base, holding the hands of their younger children. Retiree birders would stroll Charley's loop around its perimeter, ever alert for a glimpse of scarlet tanagers.

Purgatory Chasm had an exhibit-filled ranger station, a covered gazebo for picnicking, and a playground carefully floored with shock-absorbing rubber.

Here, though, there was barely a wood sign-board to give one an idea of the lay of the land. The few reservoirs deep in the forest were marked, as well as where the forest proper overlapped with the Whitinsville Water Company property. That was it. Once you headed in here you were on your own. The maze of twisty little passages, all different, were as challenging to navigate as that classic Adventure game where you would be eaten by a grue once your lantern ran out of oil. A person new to the trails would be foolhardy to head in without a GPS or perhaps a pocket full of breadcrumbs.

In the full warmth of summer I would be alert to spot a few American toads, a scattering of dragonflies, and an attentive swarm of mosquitoes. This first day of November was both better and worse. The mosquitoes had long since departed, but along with them they had taken the amphibians and fluttering creatures that I usually delighted in on my walks. I had been rambling for a full hour now and the most I had heard was the plaintive *ank-ank* cry of a nuthatch. Maybe it, too, was wondering where the smaller tasty morsels had gone off to.

Still, with the trees now bare of their leafy cover, there was much to see. The woods were usually dense with foliage, making it hard to peer even a short distance into their depths. Now it was as if a bride had removed her veil and her beauty had been revealed. The edges of a ridge against the grey-blue sky showed a delicate tracery of granite amongst the darker stone. A stand of elderly oaks was stunning, the deep creases of the sand-brown bark rivaling the wise furrows in an aged grandfather's brow.

I came around a corner and stopped in surprise. A staggeringly tall oak had apparently succumbed to the storm's fury and had fallen diagonally across the path. A thick vine traced its way along the length of the tree, adding a beautiful spiraling pattern to the bark. The tree's crown stretched far into the brush on the left, but on the right the roots had been ripped up and a way was clear around them.

I moved off the trail to circumvent this interesting new obstacle in life, eyeing the tree. When I'd parked at the trail head there had been two trucks tucked along the roadside. One had been a crimson pick-up truck with no shotgun racks or other indications of hunting, at least that I could see. With luck the owner was just out for a walk like I was. The other vehicle had been a white F-150 clearly marked as belonging to the Department of Conservation. If the ranger was in here somewhere, hopefully he'd spotted the tree and was making plans to clear the trail. If I hadn't run into him by the time I emerged I'd leave him a note on his windshield.

My foot caught on a hidden root and I stumbled, catching myself against the rough bark of a mature oak. I shook my head, brushing my long, auburn hair back from my eyes. The forest floor was coated with perhaps two inches of oak leaves in tan, chocolate, fawn, and every other shade of brown I could imagine. My usual hunt for mushrooms had been stymied by the dense, natural carpet, and I knew better than to daydream while walking through this hazard.

My eyes moved up – and then stopped in surprise.

The elderly man lay on his back as if he had decided to take a mid-day nap during his stroll. His arms were spread, his head relaxing to one side. But his eyes were wide open, staring unfocused at the sky, long past seeing anything. The crimson blossom at his chest was a counterpoint to the dark green jacket he wore. The blood was congealed, the edges dry.

My hand went into my pocket before I gave it conscious thought, and then I was blowing sharply on the whistle I carried. It was only after a long minute that my mind began to clear from the shock, to give thought to the cell phone I carried in my other pocket. For so many years the whistle had been my first resort, the quickest way to communicate with fellow hikers.

I was just reaching into my other pocket when there was the whir and crunching of an approaching mountain bike. The ranger rode hard into view along the main trail, pulling to a skidding stop at the fallen tree. He was lean and well-built, perhaps a few years older than me, wearing a bright orange vest over a jacket peppered with foresting patches. His eyes swept me with concern.

"Are you hurt, miss?" he asked, his gaze sharp and serious as he caught his breath.

I found I could not speak, could only wave a hand in the direction of the fallen body. The dead man's hair was a pepper of grey amongst darker brown. He had been handsome, in a rough-hewn older cowboy sort of way, and in good shape for his age. Had he slipped on the leaves and fallen against a cut-off tree? Stiff and spindly stumps could almost seem like punji sticks, those sharp-edged spikes that the Viet-Cong laid as traps for unwary infantrymen.

The ranger gave a short shake of his head; I realized he could not see into the ravine from his vantage point. He climbed off his bike; his sure stride brought him to my side in seconds. He pulled up suddenly as his eyes caught sight of the body, then he slid down the slope, moving to kneel at the fallen man's side. He carefully laid a finger against the neck, pausing in silence, but I knew before he dropped his gaze what he would find.

He had his cell phone to his ear in moments, twisting loose the clasp on his bike helmet, running a hand through his thick, dark brown hair. "Jason here. We have a dead body in Sutton Woods, north of Melissa's Path. Just by where I reported that downed tree earlier. Get a team in here right away." He paused for a long moment, listening, his eyes sweeping the forest around him. "No," he responded shortly. "I think he's been –"

There was the shuffling of motion from above; both of us turned suddenly at the noise. A sinewy man stood there in day-glow orange, his wrinkled face speckled with age spots, a visored hunter's cap covering wisps of silvered hair. His eyes moved between the two of us with bright concern. "I heard the whistle. Is something wrong?"

In his hands he held a Ruger 10/22 rifle, the matte barrel pointed somewhere up-trail.

Jason settled into stillness. His eyes remained steady on the older man's, his lean frame solidifying somehow into a prepared crouch. The hand holding the phone gently eased down toward his hip. "Sir, I need to ask you to place your rifle on the ground and step back."

The hunter's worn brow creased in confusion. "I don't understand –"

"Sir," repeated Jason, a steely note sliding into his request. "Put down the rifle." His hand was nearly at his hip now.

The hunter nodded, taking in the patches on Jason's shoulders, and lowered the rifle into the layer of leaves. When he stepped back, Jason moved with a speed I had not thought possible, putting himself between me and the hunter, taking up the rifle as if it was made of bamboo.

The hunter looked between us in surprise, and then his eyes drifted further, drawing in the sight below us. His face went white with shock and he staggered down to one knee. "My God! Is he dead?"

"Have you been shooting today?" asked Jason in response, moving his nose for a moment to the barrel of the gun to sniff for signs of firing.

"Yes, sure, for coyote," agreed the hunter, his voice rough. "But I'm careful! I never would've shot a *person*."

Jason glanced for a moment back at the fallen man. "He might not have been easy to see," he pointed out. "Forest green jacket, blue jeans, he could have looked like a shadowy movement."

The hunter shook his head fiercely. "Ask anyone," he stated, his voice becoming firmer. "I call them my Popovich Principles. I look three times before I even put my finger into the trigger guard. I hear too many tales of accidents. I only took three shots today, and each time my target was solid."

My throat was dry. "Were you sure of your background each time?"

He glanced up at me, and his brow creased even further. "I thought ... but I'm not sure ..."

Jason looked over to me, nodding. "We will figure that all out soon enough," he agreed. "In the meantime, miss ..."

"Morgan," I responded. "Morgan Warren. I live a few miles from here."

"Miss Warren," he echoed, an easing of tension releasing his shoulders. He rested the rifle butt-down on the forest floor. "If you don't mind, we can all wait here for the police and make sure we get all our facts straight."

I settled down cross-legged with my back against an aspen tree, breathing in the scent of juniper, and closed my eyes. After a few minutes a sense of calm resurfaced. The woods drifted toward the peaceful, quiet, eternal sense that it had possessed when I first stepped onto the trail only a short while ago.

* * *

The police had come and gone, the medics had respectfully carried away the dead body, and the forest had eased into a dark blue twilight that resembled the depths of an ocean floor. Jason had remained at my side through it all. Now he stared with me down at the empty space at the base of the ravine. The scattering of witch hazel along the edges added a faint golden glisten to the scene.

"But I didn't hear a shot," I stated finally, as if that made all the difference.

He gave his head a short shake. "Mr. Popovich began his hunting back at dawn," he pointed out. "The victim was apparently shot a few hours later. The body was long dead by the time you reached it. He was undoubtedly dead before you left your house to come here. The M.E. will let us know for sure."

"He looked asleep," I continued. My thoughts were not quite coming in a coherent fashion.

He hesitated for a moment, then put an arm around my shoulder to comfort me. "Can I take you home?"

I shook my head. I was forty-three years old. Certainly old enough to be able to cope with this situation, as unusual as it was. And my home was a mere five-minute drive.

"I'll be fine," I assured him. But it was another long minute before I could pull my eyes from the spot and turn to navigate back around the fallen tree.

"We may need to ask you follow-up questions in the coming days, as we pursue our investigation," he murmured as we made our way up the trail.

"Of course," I agreed, my eyes taking in the forest around me as if it had recently sprung to life. Every twisted branch, every fluttering oak leaf clinging tenaciously to its tree sent a small surge of adrenaline through me. I wrapped my tangerine sarong even closer around my shoulders.

Worry creased Jason's eyes, and he ran a hand through his chestnut-brown hair. I wondered for a moment where his biking helmet had gone, and then remembered the police taking it and his bike back with them at his request.

A strange sense of loss nestled in my heart; I spoke to shake it loose. "I'm sorry to have kept you behind with me."

"Not at all," he demurred with understanding in his eyes. "I was happy to stay."

I lapsed into silence again, absorbed in the soft crunch of leaves beneath my feet, in the soft whistling of the dusk breeze as it scattered through birch and aspen. Jason was steady at my side. My shoulders slowly eased as we walked along the trail.

At last the trail widened before us. I'd never seen the vehicle gate at the mouth standing open, and it brought into focus again just what had happened here. I stared at it for a long moment before bringing my eyes up to the two cars standing side by side, his white F-150, my dark-green Forester.

He fished in a side pocket and brought out a card. "If you need anything – anything at all – you just call," he offered, and his eyes were warm as he handed the card to me.

I nodded, turned, and then I was back in the safety of my car, driving toward the security of home.

Here's where to learn what happened next!

Aspen Allegations

On Amazon:

Aspen Allegations

Other platforms:

http://www.suttonmass.org/suttonmassmysteries/aspenallegations/

Thank you so much for all of your support and encouragement for this important cause.

49594201R00098

Made in the USA
Columbia, SC
24 January 2019